Wish You Weren't Here

Katie Redford

methuen | drama

LONDON • NEW YORK • OXFORD • NEW DELHI • SYDNEY

METHUEN DRAMA
Bloomsbury Publishing Plc
50 Bedford Square, London, WC1B 3DP, UK
1385 Broadway, New York, NY 10018, USA
29 Earlsfort Terrace, Dublin 2, Ireland

BLOOMSBURY, METHUEN DRAMA and the Methuen
Drama logo are trademarks of Bloomsbury Publishing Plc

First published in Great Britain 2024

Cover design by Guy J Saunders

A catalogue record for this book is available from the British Library.

A catalog record for this book is available from the Library of Congress.

ISBN: PB: 978-1-3504-7430-7
ePDF: 978-1-3504-7432-1
eBook: 978-1-3504-7433-8

Series: Modern Plays

Typeset by Mark Heslington Ltd, Scarborough, North Yorkshire

To find out more about our authors and books visit
www.bloomsbury.com and sign up for our newsletters.

Wish You Weren't Here was commissioned by Theatre Centre and is a co-production between Theatre Centre and Sheffield Theatres.

Wish You Weren't Here premiered at Tanya Moiseiwitsch Playhouse at Sheffield Theatre in January 2024.

Thanks from Katie Redford

Thank you to every single person who shared their experiences with me. To the incredible team at Theatre Centre who have provided a platform for not just me but for hundreds of young people across the country, making sure their voices are heard. To every school that opened their doors to us: Parkside Community School, Addey and Stanhope, Newfield School, Prendergast School and Bonas Pastor Catholic College. To Lewisham Youth Theatre. To the National Youth Theatre and the brilliant women who gave everything and more in our R&D. To Ben and the facilitators who orchestrated all of the workshops. To every actress who auditioned, including our wonderful cast, Eleanor and Olivia. To the entire creative team who have been working tirelessly behind the scenes. And to Rob, for constantly being the voice of reason during my moments of doubt and despair (there were a few) and for making every room feel as safe and special as they did.

Thank you to the following young people and artists who supported the development of *Wish You Weren't Here*:

Diamond Adeyemo, Sophia Andrea, Jackson Barclay, Rebecca Batcup, Ellie Blackburn, Jasmine Brown, Toto Bruin, Rivkah Bunker, Lulu Chaps, Michaela Dadzie, Dulcie Davy, Chiquita Delisser, Lashay Francis, Teyanna Green, Shueb Hassain, Keziah Hopkinson, Na'shiya Johnson Beth Knight, Rhys Knox, Ebony Komolafe, latekid, Lauren Lepperd, Naomi Lune, Emily Lysons, Ndabane Makukula, Mohamed Malik-Koroma, Scarlett Malone, Shamar Murphy, Oswald Ojelade, Lami Rosian Olopade, Liberty Onyeneke-Skinner, AFLO. the poet, Maria Ramjee, Kai Roberts, Amaarah Roze, Cherish Salami, Indi SB, Malachy Scott, Blessin Tate-Atkinson, Marguerite Vermersch, Monsikelah Ward, Enoch Zepo

THEATRE CENTRE

Founded in 1953 by Brian Way and Margaret Faulks, we've been a vital catalyst for youth leadership and creativity for 70 years.

In this time, we've commissioned 108 writers and produced 237 plays. We have played to audiences of over 1 million in schools and theatres and we have worked with over 250,000 young people through a vast range of projects. Some of those young people are now working in the arts, running companies of their own, or in education teaching drama to the next generations.

We commission new writing from trailblazing writers, touring directly into schools and theatres UK-wide, as well as running our year-round Future Makers activities to bring young people, artists, and teachers together as creative collaborators. Future Makers makes space for young people to have agency as they nurture their talent and interests on their terms.

We see access, equality, and representation as foundations of a fair society and work to dismantle exclusion and systemic injustice. We prioritise areas that are systemically underserved and excluded, removing economic and social barriers, and working where young people can benefit most. We celebrate the true creative diversity only the widest access can bring.

www.theatre-centre.co.uk

 Supported using public funding by
**ARTS COUNCIL
ENGLAND**

SHEFFIELD THEATRES

Sheffield Theatres is home to three theatres: the Crucible, the Sheffield landmark with a world-famous reputation; the Playhouse, an intimate, versatile space for getting closer to the action; and the gleaming Lyceum, the beautiful proscenium that hosts the best of the UK's touring shows.

Having held the title 'Regional Theatre of the Year' on four separate occasions, Sheffield Theatres is the ticket to big names and local heroes, timeless treasures and new voices. Committed to investing in the creative leaders of the future, Sheffield Theatres' dedicated talent development hub, The Bank, supports a new cohort of emerging theatre-makers every year.

Sheffield Theatres has a reputation for bold new work. Starting life in the Crucible in 2019, the award-winning **Life of Pi** transferred to the West End in 2021 and to Broadway in 2023. This success follows hit musical **Everybody's Talking About Jamie** which also transferred to the West End, toured the UK and enjoyed a feature film release internationally on Amazon Prime in 2021. **Everybody's Talking About Jamie** returns to Sheffield on tour in 2024. In 2022, **ROCK / PAPER / SCISSORS** was staged across all three theatres to celebrate the 50th anniversary of the Crucible and Playhouse, winning Best Directors at the UK Theatre Awards 2022. Also during the anniversary year, the acclaimed **Accidental Death of an Anarchist** opened the newly named Tanya Moiseiwitsch Playhouse in September 2022. The show transferred to the West End in June 2023, winning a UK Theatre Award in the same year. Over Christmas 2022, Sheffield Theatres, in co-production with the National Theatre and Various Productions, revived **Standing at the Sky's Edge**, returning the show to the Crucible before transferring to the Olivier Theatre and winning two Olivier awards including Best New Musical. The show transfers to the West End in February 2024. In 2023, Sheffield Theatres' productions have received five UK Theatre Award nominations, including two for their reimagined revival of **Miss Saigon**, staged by special arrangement with Cameron Mackintosh in summer 2023.

Crucible Lyceum Playhouse 55 Norfolk Street, Sheffield, S1 1DA

sheffieldtheatres.co.uk

ORIGINAL CAST AND CREATIVES

CAST

Lorna
Eleanor Henderson

Mila
Olivia Pentelow

CREATIVES

Writer
Katie Redford

Sound Designer
Tom Sharkett

Director
Rob Watt

Set and Costume Designer
Bethany Wells

Lighting Designer
Jess Brigham

Movement Director
Kiren Virdee

PRODUCTION

Marketing for Theatre Centre
Rachel Bellman

Casting Consultant
Becky Paris

Schools Tour Booking and
Co-ordination for Theatre Centre
Becky Ide

Producers for Theatre Centre
Rowan Prescott & Emma Rees

Marketing Consultants
Jane Morgan Associates

Artwork
Guy J Saunders

PR
Chloe Nelkin Consulting & Jo Allan PR

Production Manager
Brent Tan

Company Stage Manager
Laura Whittle

LORNA played by Eleanor Henderson

Eleanor trained at the Royal Conservatoire of Scotland. Theatre credits include: *Henry V* (Shakespeare's Globe); *Little Scratch* (Hampstead Theatre and New Diorama); *Blood Wedding* (Salisbury Playhouse); *Gave Her the Eye* (Soho Theatre); *I Know You Died* (Theatre503) Gate (Cockpit Theatre); *Albee Vector the Sound Collector* (UK tour); *Coriolanus* (Bard in The Botanics); *Much Ado About Nothing* (Bard in The Botanics); *The Merchant of Venice* (Shakespeare's Globe/RCS); *As You Like It* (Shakespeare's Globe/RCS); *Fagin's Last Night Alive* (West Yorkshire Playhouse); *As You Like It* (RADA Festival); *Pass It On* (Hammersmith Lyric).

TV and film credits include: *Where The Mountains Grow* (Black Apron Entertainment); *All Is Not Lost* (Affixius Films); *Seven Deadly Sins* (Discovery Channel).

MILA played by Olivia Pentelow

Olivia is a talented actor from Bradford. She has most recently appeared in *Ridley* (ITV) and *The Gallows Pole* (BBC).

Whilst with the Northern School of Creative Industries she took on the roles of Susan in *Miracle of Bradford* and Elisabeth Proctor in *The Crucible*.

Wish You Weren't Here was Olivia's professional stage debut.

Katie Redford
Writer

Katie is an award-winning writer and performer. She's a BAFTA Rocliffe Comedy TV winner and was also on the BBC Comedy Writersroom and Soho Theatre Writers Lab. Her short film *Ghosted* starring Alison Steadman, which she wrote, produced and performed in, was supported by BFI Network and Film Hub Midlands and went into commissioned development for TV. Her debut drama *Yellow Lips* aired on BBC Radio 4 in 2021 in which she also played the lead in and was nominated for The Imison Award. Her debut stage play *Tapped* premiered at Theatre503 in 2022, followed by a UK tour, for which Katie received an Offie nomination for Most Promising Playwright. She is currently a writer in residence with Theatre Centre and has projects in commissioned development for stage, TV and radio.

Rob Watt
Director

Rob Watt is a critically acclaimed director, dramaturg, and facilitator. He is currently the Artistic Director for Theatre Centre, regularly teaches at the Royal Central School of Speech and Drama and works with the Institute of the Arts Barcelona. He previously was an associate for Headlong Theatre, headed up the young people's team at the National Theatre, was a lead artist at Lyric Hammersmith, an artist mentor at the Barbican and Associate Director at Immediate Theatre.

Selected credits: *Birds and Bees* by Charlie Josephine (Theatre Centre and Sheffield Theatres, UK tour); *Human Nurture* by Ryan Calais Cameron (Theatre Centre and Sheffield Theatres, UK tour); *C+NTO* by Joelle Taylor (Apples and Snakes); *Acts of Resistance* by Stef Smith (Headlong Theatre and Bristol Old Vic); *Rallying Cry* by Apples and Snakes (BAC, BBC Contains Strong Words Festival Hull, Brighton Fringe); *Be Prepared* by Ian Bonar (Underbelly / VAULT Festival); *Party Trap* by Ross Sutherland (Shoreditch Town Hall); *Goosebumps* by Rob Watt (The Vaults); *Standby For Tape Back-Up* by Ross Sutherland (Summerhall / UK tour).

Jess Brigham
Lighting Design

Jess Brigham is a lighting designer from Hull, having recently graduated with a first class degree from Liverpool Institute for Performing Arts.

She was selected to be a member of the SLX Lighting Programme and The Godber Theatre Foundation during this time.

Recent credits include: *Identities*, directed by Maya Shimmin (Close to Home Productions, UK tour); *Innit: Musical*, directed by Micky Dacks (I4YPC, The Quays – The Lowry); *Burning Down The Horse*, directed by Maya Shimmin (Fishing 4 Chips, Pleasance Beneath – Edinburgh Fringe); *Mumsy*, directed by Zoe Waterman (Hull Truck Theatre); *Katzenmusik*, directed by Sammy Glover (London Youth Theatre, Seven Dials Playhouse); *A Sudden Violent Burst of Rain*, directed by Yasmin Hasefji (The Gate Theatre); *The True Adventures of Marian and Robin Hood*, directed by Francesca Goodridge (Barn Theatre); *Identities*, directed by Maya Shimmin (Close to Home Productions, UK tour); *End Without Days*, choreographed by Stephen Pelton (Dancebase, Edinburgh Fringe); *Much Ado About Nothing*, directed by Kayleigh Hawkins (HER Productions, Manchester Hope Mill) and *Patricia Gets Ready (for a date with the man that used to hit her)*, directed by Kaleya Baxe (UK tour, *Greatest Days*, directed by Stacey Haynes and Tim Firth (Associate Lighting Designer to Rob Casey, UK tour); *Lemons Lemons Lemons Lemons Lemons*, directed by Josie Rourke (Assistant Lighting Designer, Harold Pinter Theatre and UK tour).

Tom Shakett
Sound Design

Tom Sharkett is a producer, composer and sound designer from Manchester. Having co-founded synth-pop band W. H. Lung, with whom he has released two albums and toured the UK, USA and Europe, he has released his own productions on dance music label Optimo Music as well as remixes for other artists. Tom began working as a sound designer in theatre in 2022, and has most recently worked with the Royal Central School of Speech and Drama, Extant Theatre and Angel Exit. Tom is also currently working as an audio artist on a project exploring the connections between sound and mental health and wellbeing.

Brent Tan
Production Manager

Brent is a production manager and trained at LAMDA, majoring in production management. Brent is from Singapore and has an interest in immersive theatre and touring.

Credits include: *50 Days* (BYMT); *Prague Quadrennial* (Secretive Thing); *Home X* (Kakilang Arts); *Richard the Second* (Tangle Theatre); *Bunker of Zion* (UK tour); *Wilderness* (LAMDA); *Against* (LAMDA); *The Welkin* (LAMDA); *King Charles III* (LAMDA); *Miss Julie* (LAMDA); *Queens of Sheba* (LAMDA); *Desert Boy* (LAMDA); *WeRNotVirus2* (Moongate Theatre); *Amaterasu: Out of the Cave* (Papergang Theatre); *Fat Kids Are Harder To Kidnap* (Singapore); *StoryFest* (Singapore); *Ghost Train* (Singapore).

Bethany Wells
Set and Costume Designer

Trained in architecture, Bethany is an award-winning performance designer working across dance, theatre, and installation, with particular interest in site-specific and devised performance. She sees all her work as a form of spatial, social and sensory activism. She is interested in exploring what can be achieved politically and socially by the collective live experience of performance. Her practice is trauma-informed, in terms of both process and audience experience.

Work in development includes: *Baby, He Loves You* (Middle Child); *Wayfarers* (Claire Cunningham Projects).

Recent work includes: *All That Lives* (The Grief Series); *The People's Palace of Possibility* (The Bare Project). *You Heard Me* (Luca Rutherford); *Choreography of Care* (Claire Cunningham); *Written in the Body* (Charlotte Spencer Projects, Brighton Festival); *This Endless Sea* (Chlöe Smith); *Birds and Bees* (Charlie Josephine, Sheffield Theatres); *Thank You Very Much* (Claire Cunningham, MIF/National Theatre of Scotland).

Laura Whittle
Company Stage Manager

Laura is a freelance stage manager, specialising in small/mid-scale theatre and events. Most recently she was stage manager on the book for *The Light Princess* at the Albany. Other credits include: *Haringey Feast* (Haringey Council/Alexandra Palace); Edinburgh Fringe (Pleasance/Underbelly); *Pride in London* (Underbelly); *Tapped* (Bethany Cooper Productions/Theatre503); VAULT Festival, *La Clique* (Underbelly); Platinum Jubilee Pageant, *Bangers* (Cardboard Citizens); and *Headcase* (Blue Gravy Productions/Matthew Schmolle Productions).

Kiren Virdee
Movement Director

Kiren Virdee is a movement director, choreographer, and performing artist. She has trained in movement direction and teaching with the Royal Central School of Speech and Drama (CSSD) from which she graduated with distinction. Prior to this, she trained at Trinity Laban Conservatoire of Music and Dance from which she graduated with distinction, gaining the Audrey Wethered Award and Choreography Prize. Kiren also studied English Literature, at the University of Bristol, from which she graduated with a first.

She has worked as movement director, choreographer, artist, and facilitator in various professional, educational, and community settings. This has included work with organisations such as The Place, Siobhan Davies, CSSD, Zoo Co. Youth Co., Fourth Monkey, and the London School of Dramatic Art. Recent movement direction credits include: movement director and choreographer, *Seize the Cheese*, New Wimbledon Theatre; movement director, *Kolaja*; feature film, movement director and intimacy, *Grey Area* (Vaults, Kings Head Theatre); and movement associate, *2 Billion Beats* (Orange Tree Theatre).

Theatre Centre would like to thank the following people

To all the young people, artists and teachers from across the UK who helped develop *Wish You Weren't Here*.

Tom Bird and Rob Hastie.

Dr Adele Greaves and Beacon House.

Helena Lymbery.

Backstage Trust for their support of our Sheffield Future Makers Hub and the Garrick Trust for their support of our Resident Writers, both of which were crucial in the development of *Wish You Weren't Here*.

Our Chair Rebecca Major and Trustees Aleksa Asme, Titilola Dawudu, Frazer Flintham and David Luff.

THEATRE CENTRE TEAM

Marketing Manager
Rachel Bellman

Finance Director
David Lewis

Programme and Admin
Co-Ordinator
Becky Ide

Community Partnerships
Producer
Moni Onojeruo

Future Makers Producer
Ben Di Meo

Executive Director and CEO
Emma Rees

Artistic Director
Rob Watt

SHEFFIELD THEATRES TEAM

CEO
Tom Bird

Deputy CEO
Bookey Oshin DL

Artistic Director
Robert Hastie

SENIOR MANAGEMENT TEAM

Communications Director
Rachel Nutland

Associate Artistic Director
Anthony Lau

Customer Experience Director
Caroline Laurent

Operations Director
John Bates

Fundraising and Commercial
Director
Elizabeth Barran

Finance Director
Kathy Gillibrand

Producer
Nick Stevenson

Learning & Participation Director
Jenna Omeltschenko

ADMINISTRATION TEAM

HR Manager
Victoria Cooper

HR Advisors
Lorna Tomlinson, **Lianne
Froggatt**

Assistant to Chief Executive and
Artistic Director
Jackie Pass

SALES AND CUSTOMER EXPERIENCE TEAM

Front of House Manager
Debbie Fairest

Deputy Front of House Manager
Jake Ross

Sales Managers
Kate Fisher, Louise Renwick

Sales & Customer Care
Supervisor
Faye Marsden

Sales & Groups Supervisor
Ian Caudwell

Sales & Administration Supervisor
Charlotte Keyworth

Sales Assistants
Rebecca Alldrick, Sue Cooper, Sally Field, Julia Harrod, Mark Kelwick, Irene Stewart, Georgina Stone, Katy Wainwright

COMMUNICATIONS TEAM

Communications Manager
Oliver Eastwood

Communications Executive
Thomas Adcock

Media Officer
Carrie Askew

Communications Officer
Laura Hill

Communications Assistant
Sophie Walker

National Press
Jo Allan PR

Multimedia Producer
Lucy Smith-Jones

EVENTS AND HOSPITALITY TEAM

Events and Hospitality Manager
Kelvin Charles

Deputy Hospitality Manager
Aeddan Lockett

Casual Chefs
Natalie Bailey, Stephen Delmar-Shaw, John Forrest

Cellar Person
Robin Atkinson

Events Co-ordinator
Ellen Mutch

Hospitality Supervisors
Lucy Bytheway, Curtis Dunn, Curtis Fairest, Gregory Knowles, Harris Slater, Charles Swift

Hospitality Assistants
Maya Andrews, Kyle Baker, Olivia Barton, Phelo Bird, Nic Bowden, Grace Bower, Michael Broughton, Jessica Carter-Edwards, Anthreas Charcharos, Rose Cleary, Eve Crownshaw, Gill Crownshaw, Alison Crossfield, James

Doolan, Emily Fairhurst, Judith
Flint, Zoe Gahn, Netta Gamble,
Scott Gist, Joanne Hall,
Georgia Hatton, Emily
Haycock, Laura Hewitt,
Rosalind Hodgson, Jorja
Holmes, Sandra Holmes, Kate
Hunter, Maisy Hunter, Zoe
Jones, Holly Kempton, Zoe
Kempton, Hannah Lamare,
Peter Leigh, Megan Leybourne,
Luke Lincoln, Georgia
Lingwood, Grey Martin, Ellen
McAuley, Niamh McGregor,
Emmi Mellor, Molly Murray,
Antonia Nadragila, Eve Orange,
James O'Shea, Grace Parker-
Slater, Megan Peace, Amelia-
Daisy Phair, Ellie Platts, Louise
Platts-Dunn, Kayla Price,
Suhana Rai, Cyndi Richardson,
Clare Riley, Hollie Roberts,
Haris Sadiq, Quiana Smith, Max
Sneddon, Arabella Sumaculub,
Caryl Thomas, Sophie
Thompson, Shyla Toulalan,
Emily Toulson, Milly
Wainwright, Abigail Webster,
George Webster, Claire
Whowell

Front of House Duty Managers
**Emma Chapman, Sue Cooper,
Denise Hobart, Lucy Hockney,
Irene Stewart, Adrian Tolson,
Joe White**

Front of House Assistants
**Aminat Abari, Susan
Anderson, Anne Archer,
Stephen Athey, Martin Bailey,
Belinda Beasley, Isabel
Berriman, Marianne Bolton,**
Debra Briggs, Elizabeth
Briggs, Mari Bullock, Lorna
Byrne, Terry Byrne, Julie
Cartwright, Jane Challenger,
Oliver Cocker, Ryan Coleflax,
Yolanda Collier, Lilli Connelly,
Toby Corrigan, Nicky Crewe,
Gillian Crossland, Aimee Dack,
John Daggett, Marie Darling,
Rebecca Davison, Permjeet
Dhoot, Sandra Eddison,
Connie Fiddament, Daisy
Frossard, Anne Furniss,
Margaret Gallagher, Mark
Gaynor, Emeline Gilhooley,
Samantha Green, Shane
Greenacre, Elizabeth Halliday,
Kimberley Harris, Julia Harrod,
Christine Heery, Nick Henry,
Gregory Higginson, Jacqueline
Homer, Scott Johnson, Alex
Lamb, Martha Lamb, Diane
Lilleyman, Margaret Lindley,
Emilia Lodge, Balazs Maro,
Laura Marsh, Gabriel Mason,
Christine Monaghan, Stasha
Moutzouris, Susan Newman,
Catherine Oldham, Louise
Owen, Holly Parker, Claire
Pass, Ann Phenix, Heather
Reynolds, Cameron
Saunderson, Isobel
Simmonite, Sabrina Soar,
Georgina Stone, Sharon Stone,
Nell Tomlinson, Vanesa
Trifkovic, Beverley Turner,
Christine Wallace

Fire Persons
**Connie Fiddament, Julia
Harrod, Rebecca Hill, Susanne
Palzer, Lucy Richards**

FACILITIES AND TECHNICAL TEAM

Operations Manager
Julius Wilson-Wolfe

Head of Maintenance
Julian Simpson

Maintenance Technician
Richard Powell-Pepper

Operations Office
Martin Bailey

House Supervisor
Taz Taylor

House Assistants
Andrew Battey, Shane Greenacre, David Hayes, Joseph Ross, Cameron Saunderson, Shannon Stockley, Olivia T'Gan Swords, Richard Winks

Casual House Assistant
Josh Allen

Head Cleaner
Tracey Kemp

Deputy Head Cleaner
Pamela Jackson

Cleaners
Louisa Cottingham, Yvonne Dwyer, Gail Fox, Ken Kamara, Tapiwa Mwamuka, Troy Nurse, Carl Phipps, Andrew Roberts, Diane Sayles, Alan Scott, Cecilia Sidi, Diane Turton, Karen Walker

Technical Operations Manager
Gary Longfield

Head of Lighting
Neale Franklin

Deputy Head of Lighting
Chris Brown

Lead Lighting Technician
Kati Hind

Lighting Technicians
Tobias Leadbitter, Connor O'Neil

Head of Sound & Video
Nick Greenhill

Deputy Head of Sound & Video
Adam Griggs

Head of Stage
James Turner

Deputy Head of Stage
Dave Pumford

Lead Stage Technician
Chris Platts

Stage Technicians
Dan Stephens, Tom Whittaker

Theatre Technicians
Hin Cheung Edmond Lee, Paulina Chochulska, Sean Collins

Technical Apprentice
Elinor Henson

Head of Workshop
Nathan King

Casual Lighting Crew
Phil Baines, Nicholas Clayton, Peter Conn, Zoe Edwards, Chris Ellis, Matthew Ellis, Rachel Eyton, Ambra Fuller, Jodi Garth, Chris Hanlon, Nick Johnson, Paul Minott, James Reynolds, Sophie Slater, Andy Sulley

Casual Stage Crew
Dan Alexander, Charlotte Dale, Callum Ditchburn, Chris Ellis,

Matthew Ellis, **Kai Falkowski**, **Alex Hackett**, **Chris Hanlon**, **Euan Irving**, **Philip Lee**, **Robert Lee**, **Matt Orme**

Security Officer
James Harland

FINANCE TEAM

Finance Manager
James Hancock

Payroll & Finance Officer
Jean Deakin

Finance Officer
Lesley Barkworth-Short

Finance Apprentice
Alex Clayton

FUNDRAISING TEAM

Individual Giving Officer
Leah Woffenden

Trust and Partnerships
Development Officer
Adam Battey

Membership Co-ordinator
Claire Fletcher

LEARNING TEAM

Learning Co-ordinator
Sam Erskine

Workshop and Project Assistants
Eleanor Blackburn, Alice Connolly, Connie Fiddament, Ashley Gregory, Ruth Lee, Morven Robinson, Noor Sobka

Community Engagement Officer
Simon Marshall

Participation Co-ordinator
Dawn Richmond-Gordon

PRODUCING TEAM

Consultant Producer
Matthew Byam Shaw

Assistant Producer
Mitchell Vernals

Artistic Associates
Chris Bush, Wendy Spon, Caroline Steinbeis

Programmer
Laura Bloor

Production Manager
Stephanie Balmforth

Company Manager
Andrew Wilcox

Stage Manager
Sarah Gentle

New Work Co-ordinator
Ruby Clarke

Deputy Stage Manager
Sarah Greenwood

Talent Development Co-ordinator
Tommi Bryson

Producing & Learning Assistant
Rosalind Moore

Agent for Change
Richard Peralta

Head of Wardrobe
Debbie Gamble

Deputy Heads of Wardrobe
Abi Nettleship, Sally Wilson

Wardrobe Assistants
Hannah Dumm, Rose Jennings, Eleanor McBurnie, Merle Richards-Wright

Wardrobe & Wig Mistress
Valerie Atkinson

Dressers
Gemma Anderson, Jess Atkinson, Ella Claydon, Abigail Hindley, Hayley McCready, Jennifer Moore, Angela Platts, Katy Scott, Anouchka Santella, Amanda Thompson

Cutters
Silivia Devilly, Kate Harrison, Imogen Singer

COMPANY IN RESIDENCE

Utopia Theatre

Producer / Creative Director
Mojisola Elufowoju

SHEFFIELD THEATRES TRUST BOARD

LYCEUM THEATRE BOARD

LEARNING & PARTICIPATION COMMITTEE

FUNDRAISING COMMITTEE

'I wish adults knew . . .'

. . . how hard it is to be young these days.

. . . how easily they influence us.

. . . that if you have a messy room you know where everything is.

(Year 9 students, anonymous)

Wish You Weren't Here

Characters

Lorna, *F, white, 32.*
Mila, *F, mixed race, 16.*

All action is set in Scarborough.

/ indicates an interruption.

Friday

1

Sea front

Lorna *is attempting a selfie. She experiments with a few angles before finding the right one.*

Mila's *typing on her phone.*

Lorna *smiles for the camera.*

Lorna (*whilst smiling*)   Mila.

Mila *looks up and poses for the camera.* **Lorna** *is more smiley than* **Mila**.

Lorna *holds off on taking it, searching for a different angle.*

Mila (*whilst posing*)   Mum.

Lorna   Sorry, it's just – the arcades look a bit tacky. Think it'd be better with the sea in the –

They shuffle around so the sea is behind them. **Lorna** *takes the selfie and instantly looks at the photo.*

Mila *goes back to typing on her phone.*

Lorna   Why don't we do a fun one, like –

Lorna *pulls a 'fun face'.*

Mila   No.

Lorna   OK, let's just say 'Happy Holiday' –

They both pose. **Lorna** *is much more enthusiastic than* **Mila**.

Lorna   Happy holiday!

Mila   Happy holiday.

2

B&B bedroom

Lorna *covers* **Mila**'s *eyes. She unveils their room.*

Lorna   Ta da!

Mila's *underwhelmed.*

Lorna   Premium!

Lorna *inspects the space.*

It's quite big, innit? You can do this . . . and this . . .

She moves around the space.

Mila   There's a pube.

Lorna   Where?

Mila *gestures to the bed.*

Lorna *blows it away.*

Mila   You said it was a premium room.

Lorna   You still get pubes in premium rooms, Mila.

Mila *pulls a face.*

Lorna   B & B's always have pubes. They're forever finding them on Four in a Bed.

Mila *goes back to her phone.*

Lorna *spots the kettle and lets out a little squeal.*

Lorna   PG Tips . . . custard creams . . . little milks that aren't milks . . . it's like an all-inclusive.

Lorna *gasps.*

Lorna   Look at the view!

Mila   Tesco car park?

Lorna   No – behind that. The sea!

Mila   Where?

Lorna   There! You just have to –

They both adjust themselves to see the sea. It's quite an effort.

Do you remember that massive inflatable flamingo you used to take in the sea?

Mila   Janet?

Lorna   Janet! You used to bob about on Janet for hours.

Mila *half smiles.*

Lorna *gasps.*

Lorna   And we've got a tele . . .!

Mila *switches it on.*

Mila   We're not in Victorian times, course we've got a tele.

Lorna   Yeah, but you know what Monobrow Bob's like. Took him years to even put kettles in these rooms.

Lorna *switches it off.*

You didn't come for a weekend in Scarborough to watch Homes Under the Hammer.

Mila   Didn't come for much else.

Lorna   Right, come on! What do you want to do? World's our oyster.

Mila *pulls a face.*

Lorna   Scarborough's like the new Disneyland, there's loads to do!

Mila   Like what? And don't say crazy golf.

Lorna   Arcades . . . the fair . . .

Lorna *brings out a bucket and spade from her bag.*

The beach!

Mila *pulls a face.*

You love a sandcastle.

Mila   I did. When I was like, eight.

Lorna   This is the one you had when you were eight!

Mila   As if you've kept it.

Lorna   Still does its job!

Mila *goes back to her phone.*

And then tomorrow night, I thought we could celebrate . . .

Lorna *struggles to contain her excitement.*

Guess where I've booked.

Mila   McDonald's.

Lorna   Can't actually book McDonald's.

Mila   Beefeater.

Lorna   Nope.

Mila   Toby Carvery?

Lorna   Aim a bit higher.

. . .

Lorna   Gino's!

Mila   Where the hell's Gino's?

Lorna   That place Auntie Claire was talking about. The posh one past Peasholme Park with really thick napkins and menus that look like books.

Mila   Is that in our budget?

Lorna   YOLO. (*Explaining.*) You only live / once –

Mila   I know what YOLO is, Mum.

Lorna   Thought you'd like it.

Mila   I told you, I don't want to celebrate.

Lorna   Tough.

Lorna *brings out a bottle of prosecco from her suitcase.*

Mila   It's half twelve.

Lorna   Courtney and that lot are already on the G&T cans.

Mila   Can you stop following Courtney on Instagram. It's so weird.

Lorna   It's not weird!

Mila   It is.

Lorna   I'm not one of those embarrassing mums though, am I? Not like Amber's mum. 'Hashtag daughter hashtag love hashtag bestthingthateverhappenedtome.' She embarrasses me and I barely know the woman.

Lorna *grabs some mugs, ready to pour the bubbles.*

Mila   I don't want any.

Lorna   But we're celebrating!

Mila   You don't even know what I got!

Lorna   Tell me then.

Go on. It'll be like ripping off a plaster. '4As3Bs2Cs1D' / Bam. Done.

Mila   They're not letters anymore, Mum, they're numbers. Keep up.

Lorna   Even if you've not done great, you can still do stuff! I've done alright.

Mila   No offence but I don't really fancy a call centre.

Lorna   Don't be a snob.

Mila   I'm just saying, I've got ambitions.

Lorna   What, and I don't?

Mila   Whatever, I'm having a nap.

Lorna   We've only just got here.

Mila   So? Nan always used to have a nap as soon as she got here.

Lorna   Yeah. Because she was a nan.

Mila *lies down on the bed.*

Lorna   Fine.

Lorna *puts the bottle of prosecco away.*

Mila *spots something next to her and groans.*

Lorna   What?

Mila   Another pube.

3a

Arcades

Mila *and* **Lorna** *are on a dance mat. 'Mucho Mambo Sway' by Shaft plays. They're both concentrating profusely, but their stamping / general movement is out of sync with each other.*

3b

Arcades

Mila*'s on the slot machines.* **Lorna** *takes her surroundings in; a kid in a candy shop.*

Lorna   It always feels like Las Vegas in here!

Mila   How would you know what Las Vegas feels like? You've never even been on a plane.

Lorna *goes to object.*

Mila   And Glasgow doesn't count.

Mila *concentrates profusely.*

Mila   Think I might be addicted to gambling.

Lorna   I once spent £7 in 2p's because I had my heart set on a rubber shaped like a mushroom.

Mila   Did you get it?

Lorna   Yeah, but I lost it on the fair that afternoon. I was absolutely gutted.

Lorna *starts videoing* **Mila**.

Mila   What you doing?

Lorna   So you can show your friends you're not wallowing. Look like you're having a nice time – do a little laugh.

Mila   No!

Mila *gestures for her to stop videoing.* **Lorna** *stops.*

Lorna   Didn't realise how many of them were going this weekend. I swear there were about twenty of them on the photo Courtney posted. Where are they all gonna sleep?

Mila   Courtney's auntie's away so they're all crashing at her house.

Lorna   Courtney's auntie's got a *house*? In *London?* What the hell does she do?

Mila   Dentist.

Lorna *pulls a face.*

Mila   Some of the boys are staying in a Travel Lodge though.

Lorna   Where abouts?

Mila   King's Cross.

Lorna (*disgusted*)   King's Cross?!

Mila (*exasperated*)   Yes, King's Cross.

Lorna   Not very scenic.

Mila   They're not going to London for the rolling hills.

Lorna   What are they going for?

Mila   Just want to celebrate results.

Lorna   I know the feeling.

She playfully prods **Mila**.

Lorna   Bizarre place to celebrate. It's so miserable there. You never see anyone laughing in London.

Mila   Whereas in Sheffield everyone walks round in stitches?

Lorna   I hate London. It's too busy . . . no one talks to you . . .

Mila   Nothing to do with the fact Dad lives there.

Lorna   He doesn't live in *London*. He lives in *Surbiton*.

Mila   That is London.

Lorna   It's Surrey.

Mila *continues putting pennies in*.

Lorna   I didn't realise Max was going.

Mila   So?

Lorna   You could have gone you know. If you really wanted to.

Mila *looks at her.*

Mila   Seriously?

Lorna   What?

Mila   You lost your mind when I mentioned it.

Lorna   Yeah, well Monobrow Bob / wouldn't give me a refund!

Mila   Wouldn't give you a refund.

Mila *goes back to the slots.*

Lorna   Also, I wanted us to have some quality time
together. Feel a bit like we've not had any lately. What with –

Oh my god.

She hides behind **Mila**.

Mila   What?

Lorna   There's a guy who works here. Over there. Kissed
him years ago, behind that grabber machine.

Lorna *peers through the machines at him.*

All I could hear whilst we were kissing was the Postman Pat
theme tune on repeat from one of those little rides. His
name was like Jez . . . or Jaz, or Bez?

Lorna *looks on her phone.*

I think I might follow him on Insta.

Mila   Why are you saying 'Insta'?

Lorna   Can you stop going on like I'm some geriatric that's
been let out for the day?

Lorna *looks up.*

Oh my god, he's looking.

Lorna *smiles to him. She waves coyly.*

Can you believe that?

Mila's *concentrating on the slots.*

Lorna   Mila?

Mila   What?

Lorna   That he recognises me? After all this time?

Mila   Surely it's not been *that* long.

Lorna   It's been *years*.

Mila   You've not changed that much.

Lorna (*pleased*)   Have I not?

Mila   You've just got more lines.

Lorna   What lines?

Mila   Round here.

Mila *gestures to her eyes.*

Lorna   They're laughter lines. From laughing.

Mila   But you don't laugh.

Lorna   I laugh all the time!

Beat.

Mila.

Mila (*impatiently*)   What?

Lorna   I have *fun.*

Mila   Yeah, but you don't really laugh.

Lorna *goes to protest but gets distracted.*

Lorna   Quick – how do I look?

Mila (*without looking*)   Fine.

Lorna   Need to do better than fine. He's coming over.

4

Fairground

Mila's *on FaceTime and has her AirPods in.* **Lorna**'s *at a stall, playing a game.*

Mila   Is it? (*Laughs.*) No way . . . yeah, go on then . . . (*She waves.*) hiiiii . . . oh my days, what is Tai wearing? (*She laughs.*) Such a joker . . . is that a pool table? . . . shiiiit . . . (*She becomes slightly more mundane.*) Yeah, it's fine . . . it's quite sunny but . . . at the fair. Yeah, hang on. (*She turns the phone round to show the fair.*) Dodgems. Waltzers. Helter skelter. Cyclone – something. My mum –

Lorna *instantly abandons her game and responds.*

Lorna   Hi Courtney! How's the 'big smoke'?!

Mila *instantly moves the phone back.*

Mila (*to* **Lorna**)   Alright, calm down (*To Courtney.*) Listen, I'm gonna – yeah . . . OK, laters. Bye bye bye.

Lorna   They look like they're having fun.

Mila *sulks.*

Lorna   There'll be plenty more times you can go away with them.

Mila   No there won't. Not now everyone's going to college.

Lorna   Not all of them are.

Mila   Most of them.

Lorna   You'll make new friends.

Mila   I don't want new friends. It's literally the end.

Lorna   It's not literally the end, is it? You're not on your death bed.

Mila *continues to sulk.*

Lorna   Right, come on! Pick a ride. Any ride.

Mila   Ferris wheel?

Lorna   No chance.

Mila   You know you're more likely to die in a car crash than on a Ferris wheel.

Lorna   Lucky for us I can't drive then.

Mila   You're the only mum I know who can't drive. It's literally crazy.

Lorna   Can you stop saying literally in a non-literal sense?

Mila   Nan would have gone on the Ferris wheel with me. She loved the Ferris wheel.

Lorna *tries to lighten the mood.*

Lorna (*hinting*)   I might not be able to drive legally, but I'm pretty nifty in a dodgem . . .

Mila   It's weird you never learnt.

Lorna   It's never affected you.

Mila   Only because Nan drove me everywhere.

Lorna   No, she didn't.

Mila   She did.

Lorna   She didn't.

Mila   She did.

Lorna   OK, well, she can't now, can she, so.

Beat.

It was around here I lost that mushroom rubber.

Mila   Going on like you've got PTSD, Mum, it was a rubber.

Lorna   That I'd spent a whole hour trying to win! I tried telling myself that I'd given it a better life even if it was short lived.

Mila *looks blankly at her.*

Lorna   Because mushrooms have awful lives, don't they?

Mila   What are you on about?

Lorna   Because of the mushroom farms.

Mila *continues to look blank.*

Lorna   Mushrooms are kept on mushrooms farms, shut away with no day light and they just get a load of shit – like, actual poo – chucked all over them, day in, day out. Imagine that. Being shit on every single day. Poor little mushrooms.

Still blank.

Lorna   Right, dodgems!

Mila   Mum / listen –

Lorna *spots the sign for the dodgems.*

Lorna   Four tokens you need for them! *Four.* Used to be one. Inflation's cruel.

Mila   Mum –

Lorna   I don't want to be alive the day a Freddo costs more than 50p.

Mila   I've brought Nan.

Lorna   What?

Mila   I've brought her with us.

Lorna *stares at her.*

Mila   I just thought . . . she loved it here, didn't she? So, she might want to come back. For good.

Mila *brings out a sandwich bag full of ashes.*

Lorna   Is this a joke?

Mila   What?

Lorna   What the fuck's she doing in a sandwich bag?

Mila   The urn's dead heavy. This way, she can come everywhere with us.

Lorna   Mila!

Mila   What?

Lorna   Oh my god. This isn't right!

Mila   Why?

Lorna   Was – was there not anything else you could have put it in? Something less . . . see through?

Mila   *Her.* Not it.

Lorna *stares at the sandwich bag.*

Mila   I did think about putting her in my pencil case, but I was scared she'd get caught in the zip.

Beat.

I thought you'd like her being here.

Lorna   What made you think that?

Mila   Like old times.

Lorna   Does Auntie Claire know about this?

Mila   Yeah. She said it was a good idea.

Lorna (*under her breath*)   Course she fucking did.

Mila   I'll keep her safe.

Lorna   What if it flies out on the dodgems?

Mila   *She* won't.

Lorna   What . . . and you want to . . .?

Lorna *does an action with her hand.*

Mila   Don't do that.

Lorna   What?

Mila   Looks like . . .

Penny drops.

Lorna   No, I'm scattering – that (*She does it again.*) is scattering –

Mila   Can you stop? That woman's looking –

Lorna   Yeah, she's probably looking because we're standing here with a sandwich bag full of ashes –

Mila   No, it's because you look like you're . . . (*wanking*)

Lorna   No, this is more wanking. (*She gestures wanking.*)

Mila   Mum! Not in front of Nan!

Lorna   Mila, you do know that's not her.

Mila *puts her hand up to stop her mum talking.*

Lorna   Ashes are / just –

Mila   Shut up then.

Beat.

Lorna   We better not need four tokens for Nan to come on the dodgems too. I'm not made of money.

Lorna *nudges* **Mila** *playfully.*

Lorna   That was just a joke about –

Mila (*not impressed*)   The dead.

Lorna   Yep.

5

Beach

Lorna *and* **Mila** *are eating chips on the beach.* **Mila** *takes out the sandwich bag of ashes and places it in front of them.*

Lorna (*uneasy*)   Do you have to keep it in that?

Mila   What?

Lorna   It's just so . . . transparent.

I keep thinking you're bringing out a sausage roll.

Mila   Nan loved a chippy tea on the beach.

They sit in silence for a moment.

Lorna (*carefully*)   Mila . . . you can say no obviously, but . . . would it be alright if I met the man from the arcade tonight? Just for a drink.

Mila   Whatever.

Lorna   I promise I won't be long. Just a quickie. (*Realising.*) As in a quick drink. Not a quick –

Mila   Yep.

Beat.

Lorna   How's it going with Max . . .?

Mila   Don't do that.

Lorna   What?

Mila   That weird voice you do when you talk to me about boys.

Lorna   I don't do a weird voice!

Mila (*does a weird voice*)   'How's it going with Max?'

Lorna   I don't sound like that!

They smirk.

Seems to be enjoying himself in London.

Mila *stops eating.*

Mila   Why are you saying that?

Lorna   Just from Courtney's Instagram.

Mila   You better not have commented.

Lorna   I haven't!

Mila   I swear down, if you've commented –

Lorna   I haven't!

Mila   Amber's mum commented on one of Kadeem's posts like, 'Looking good boys' and she spelt boys with a z and everyone ripped her for like, ever.

Lorna   Teenagers are so cruel.

Mila   How is that cruel?!

Lorna   She's just saying they look good!

Mila   No, Mum. No.

Beat.

Lorna   So are you and Max . . . official, or –

Mila *shrugs.*

Lorna   Look, if you want my advice –

Mila   I don't –

Lorna   If you like each other, crack on.

Mila   You don't get it.

Lorna   Try me.

Mila *sighs, unsure whether to continue.*

Mila   We were seeing each other, but then . . . when Nan got ill . . . I dunno . . . I basically ghosted him . . . and yeah, now it's sort of just fizzled out.

Lorna   Do you want it to fizzle out?

Mila (*quietly*)   No.

Lorna   Reel him back in then.

Mila *looks at her mum.*

Lorna   You can't sit back with these things.

Lorna *gestures to* **Mila**'*s phone.*

Lorna   Show him what he's missing. Cheeky little photo. Trust me.

Mila *digests this.*

Lorna   Actually, let's have a nice one with our chips.

Lorna *takes a selfie of them and instantly looks at the photo.*

You don't smile enough.

Mila   Clearly enjoying my chips too much.

Lorna   Stop eating so we can have a nice photo with our chips.

Mila *does as she's told and they both smile for the photo.*

6

B&B bedroom

Lorna*'s getting ready for her date. They're listening to music (something like 'I Like It' by Cardi B). They're subtly dancing to it.*

Mila   Are you nervous?

Lorna   Nah. He'll chat about the weather, wear too much aftershave and if I mention football, he'll want to marry me. I know everything there is to know about men, trust me.

Mila   Alright, Billy Big Balls. No one likes a know it all.

Lorna *smiles proudly.*

Mila   Have you ever farted on a date?

Lorna (*horrified*)   No! I have not.

Mila   Courtney said when her and Elijah went to Nando's, he farted whilst they were eating. Said it put her off her piri piri chicken.

Lorna (*in disbelief*)   Shut up.

Mila   Right? It's something you do when you're like, married.

Lorna   I've never farted in front of a man.

Mila   What?!

Lorna *shakes her head.*

Mila   It's a perfectly natural thing to do, you know. Maybe not in Nando's, but.

Lorna   I'm just not a very . . . windy person.

Mila *scoffs.*

Lorna   I'm not!

Mila   What about that time you farted in Matalan?

Lorna   Oh my G – I did not fart in Matalan. It was / the till.

Mila   The till. Yeah, alright.

Lorna   It was!

Mila *laughs.*

Mila   Where's your top from?

Lorna   Charity shop.

Mila's *impressed.*

Lorna   Shall we do a TikTok?

Mila   No.

Lorna   Why not? You did one with Nan.

Mila   Yeah, for jokes, because she called them TokTiks.

Lorna   We always used to do dance routines together.

Mila   When I was little!

Lorna   You were my little band mate.

Lorna *puts on a track.* **Mila**'s *amused when* **Lorna** *starts getting into it. They dance in sync, although* **Lorna** *is more enthusiastic. They've clearly danced to it together before.*

Mila   Did you and Dad ever dance together?

Lorna *stops the music.*

Lorna   We were kids.

Mila   Kids dance.

Lorna *ignores her.*

Mila   You and Zoe are so different. She never like, flaps, or . . .

Lorna   That's because she's got nothing to flap about. Apart from things like ordering flat whites and what time Oliver Bonas opens.

Mila   Zoe's started practicing body positivity with me.

Lorna (*mocks*)   Alright, Lizzo.

Mila   We stand in the mirror, and she'll list all the things she likes about herself and then I'll do the same.

Lorna's *prickly.* **Mila** *places herself next to her in the mirror.*

Mila   So . . . I like my ears . . . and my wrists . . . and I suppose my eyes are quite cool too. Your turn.

Lorna   Sorry, I'm late for Jez . . .? Jaz? Baz? Shit, I really should know his name.

Lorna *blows her a kiss and leaves.*

Once **Lorna**'s *gone,* **Mila** *takes a second before meeting herself in the mirror again. She holds her phone up and starts to pose, framing different parts of her body in various ways – the poses are very subtle but it's clear she's trying to be seductive.*

7a

Bar

Lorna's *at a table.* **Mila** *rushes over to her, flustered.*

Mila   Are you OK? What's happened?

Lorna   You won't believe it.

Mila (*panicked*)   What?

Lorna   He had an apple juice.

Mila   Sorry?

Lorna   An apple juice. On a Friday night. Did not predict that.

They do cocktails if you want one. I've just had a Leg Wobbler.

Mila   You said to get here as soon as I could.

Lorna   Yeah, Happy Hour ends at half past.

Mila   It's Wetherspoons. It's always Happy Hour.

Lorna (*excited*)   Oh yeah!

Mila   I thought you were in danger, Mum. I thought – I thought – it wasn't going well.

Lorna   It wasn't going well. He had an apple juice.

Mila   I'm going back.

Lorna *grabs her arm.*

Lorna   No, please! You've only just got here! And I haven't been out in ages. With anyone. Please.

Mila *reluctantly perches on a seat.*

Lorna   God, Mila, he was so boring. He went on and on about how terrified he is of a 'cashless society' and what it'll mean for the slot machine industry, and I was sitting there, thinking I much preferred it when Postman Pat was drowning him out.

Lorna *studies the menu.*

Right. Let's get you a (*Puts on a posh voice.*) beverage . . . They do mocktails if you prefer one of those?

Mila   I'm fine.

Lorna   Your mates are downing shots playing I Have Never and you don't even want a Virgin Ginny from The Block?

Mila *rolls her eyes.*

Lorna   Look, you're here now so you may as well have something.

Mila   I'll have an oat latte.

Lorna   An *oat latte*? On a Friday night? In Wetherspoons?

Mila   Yes.

Lorna   They don't do oat milk here.

Mila   Yes, they do.

Lorna   No, they don't.

Mila   You're just too embarrassed to ask for it.

Lorna   Well, it's not milk, is it?

Mila   How is it not milk?

Lorna   You don't milk an oat, do you?

Mila   Do you know how damaged the dairy industry is?

Lorna   Can we just have one week off from climate change?

Mila   Why, is climate change having a week off?

Lorna   We're on holiday!

Mila   I had an oat latte every day when I went to Portugal with Dad and Zoe.

Lorna *slurps her drink.*

Mila   We had all-you-can-eat breakfasts that had a chocolate fountain and pancakes with any type of syrup you wanted. And they had this amazing swimming / pool that –

Lorna   The beaches are shit in Portugal.

Mila   The beaches are insane in Portugal.

Lorna   Some of them have black sand. It's weird.

Mila   It's not weird, it's eroded volcanic material.

Lorna   Yeah, well, some of us can't just swan off around the world.

Mila   Dad works hard. He doesn't just swan off.

Lorna   *I* work hard.

Mila   Did I say you didn't?

Silence.

Lorna   Blink twice if you got Cs . . .

Mila   I've told you, they're numbers now! Why do you care so much anyway?

Lorna   Because! New beginnings!

Mila   They're just another societal pressure I've not asked for.

Lorna   A cocktail will take the edge off. Something with a bit of fizz?

Mila   Fine, a sparkling water.

Lorna   You're about to reveal your GCSE results / and you want a sparkling water.

Mila   I mean, I'm not but –

Lorna   Who even drinks sparkling water?

Mila   Me.

Lorna   It's like a drinking a burp. I'm literally letting you have alcohol.

Mila   And I don't want any.

Lorna   What about a mojito? That's got mint in it so it's healthy. Or what about a shot?

Mila   No!

Lorna   Just a little one?

Mila   All shots are little.

Lorna   You can get nice ones now like strawberry tequilla. Tastes a bit like Calpol.

Mila   I'm gonna call Childline in a minute.

Lorna   You don't have enough fun, you.

(*To the bartender.*) Excuse me? Hi, yeah, can I get a sparkling water . . . (*Trying to be discreet.*) and two shots?

7b

Bar

Lorna *has been drinking quite a lot. It's now louder and rowdier in the bar.*

Lorna   I never felt like I could talk to my mum about stuff like boys and that, so I want you to feel like you can.

Mila *squirms.*

Lorna   Is there anything you want to know? About sex or . . .?

Mila   Nope.

Lorna   My first ever date –

Mila *puts her head in her hands.*

Lorna   I went to the cinema with this lad, Joe, year above me at school, and just before the film started, he put his arm round me, grabbed my boob, and in front of everyone, really loudly, shouted 'Honk honk'.

Lorna *laughs.*

Mila   Mum, that's assault.

Lorna *rolls her eyes.*

Lorna   OK.

Mila   What do you mean 'OK'?

Lorna   Well, everything's classed as assault now, isn't it?

Mila *glares at her mum.*

Lorna   I'm sorry but a man practically grazes past you at the bus stop and it's all 'hashtag me too'.

Mila   Are you serious?

Lorna   I like it when a man pips his horn at me. It's nice to feel noticed. What's wrong about that?

Mila   It's derogatory.

Lorna   It's flattering.

Mila *disapproves.*

Lorna   It's alright for you! You can have any lad you want. You're young and . . . free . . .

Mila   So are you. Sort of.

Lorna *scoffs.*

Lorna   I had a child and . . . disappeared!

Lorna *slurps her drink.*

Why is everyone so boring? No one's dancing . . .

Mila   If you wanted a big weekend, why didn't you just go away with your mates?

Lorna   Because they're all busy with their (*Mocking.*) babies. Every time I suggest doing something with them, they're like, oh we can't, we've got baby yoga or baby massage, or baby sensory, and I'm like, god, you used to be fun! When *I* was changing nappies, they were all having *their* fun, doing shots in Revolution and getting fingered at foam parties and now it's *my* turn, it's like, where is everyone?! And even when we do meet up, being a mum is *all* they talk about. And they're all doing those sickly Instagram posts, like 'Welcome to the world, Evie, Mummy and Daddy love you so much, our world is complete'. Yeah alright, give it a few years when Daddy gets bored and buggers off.

Mila   Dad didn't get bored.

Lorna   He left.

Mila   Yeah, because you guys weren't happy.

Lorna   Just because you're unhappy, Mila, doesn't mean you get to leave.

Mila   He came back every weekend.

Lorna *applauds.*

Lorna   What a hero.

Mila   He never talks about you like this.

Lorna   Like what?

Mila   Like, in a negative way. He's just . . . happy.

Lorna   *I'm* happy.

Lorna *slurps her drinks.*

And don't even get me started on parents who address Instagram posts to the baby, as if the baby is reading it. Unless they've made an actual Instagram account for the baby, which is just . . . I mean, have they asked their permission? What if the baby doesn't want to be on Instagram? But as long as everyone can see they're all going to live happily ever after, what else matters, right? Cheers to them.

Lorna *downs the last bit of her drink.*

Mila   You've never asked my permission. To put up photos of me.

Lorna   You're not a baby.

Mila   So? You still take my photo and upload it without my consent. For the world to see.

Lorna   It's not exactly the world, is it? I've got about 200 followers.

Mila   What if one's a paedophile?

Lorna   Fortunately for you, I don't know any paedophiles.

Mila   Not really how it works.

Lorna   Can we not talk about paedophiles whilst we're on holiday?

Lorna *slurps her drink, even though it's empty.*

Shall we have a dance?

Mila   No.

Lorna   Go on. Dance with me. My little band mate.

Lorna *tries to dance with* **Mila** *but she shoves her off.*

Lorna   Problem with you is that you don't dance enough.

Lorna *dances alone.*

8

Street

Mila *and* **Lorna** *are walking home.* **Lorna***'s drunk. She poses against a poster that has an image of a woman in a bikini, with the caption, 'Beach Body Ready?' across it.*

Mila   No.

Lorna   Please!

Mila   Not in front of that.

Lorna   *Her.* Not that, *her.*

Mila   I'm not taking your photo next to that.

Lorna   What, a woman?

Mila   That has the tiniest waist, the whitest skin and the biggest boobs.

Lorna   I know. Bitch.

Lorna *squints.*

Lorna   If you squint . . . she looks a bit like Courtney.

Mila   How can they get away with that? Like, who even put that up there?

Lorna   The advertising . . . people. (*Off* **Mila***'s look.*) Not everything needs questioning, Mila.

Mila   How does that not need questioning? I look nothing like her. Does that mean I'm not ready for the beach?

Lorna   If it bothers you, don't look at it.

Lorna *shields* **Mila***'s eyes.* **Mila** *shoves her off.*

Mila   Top advice, Mother.

Lorna (*stern*)   Don't call me that.

Beat.

Makes me feel old.

Mila   What's wrong with feeling old?

Lorna   Shhh.

Mila   Why can't a woman feel old?

Lorna   No more questions.

Mila   Why?

Lorna   Because it's Friday night!

Mila   And?

Lorna   And you're ruining it.

9

B&B bathroom

Lorna's *got her head in the toilet. She's drunk and very tired.*

Mila *is on the floor next to her.*

Lorna   Think we made Monobrow Bob angry . . .

Mila   *You* made him angry. Don't bring me into this.

Lorna   Some people happen to like being serenaded to.

Mila   Yeah, well, not Monobrow Bob. And not at midnight.

Lorna   Pfft.

Bet he'd order a stupid apple juice too.

Jez . . . Jaz . . . Bez . . . still don't know his name.

Lorna *retches.* **Mila** *holds her hair back.*

Lorna   When you were little, you used to hold my hand all the time. But then you grew up . . . and . . .

Beat.

Can't actually remember the last time someone held my hand.

Lorna *holds out her hand to* **Mila**. *She declines.*

Mila   You've got a bit of sick on them.

Saturday

10

Sea front

Mila *is holding a small seaside bucket. She's walking ahead of* **Lorna**, *who is hungover.*

Mila　Mum! Come on!

Lorna　Why do seagulls have to be so loud?

Mila *holds the bucket up.*

Mila　I thought you'd be pleased.

Lorna　Why would I be pleased?

Mila　It's less transparent.

Lorna　I mean, I'd prefer it if you weren't carrying around a bucket load of ashes, but . . .

Lorna *is struggling.*

Lorna　My head is pounding. I need to sit down for a minute.

She sits down on a bench.

Mila　I told you, you should have drunk that pint of water.

They sit in silence for a moment. **Lorna** *takes in the bay.*

Lorna　Have I ever told you about the little café that was up there?

Mila *shakes her head.*

Lorna　It used to be up on that hill. You'd have to scramble up all these rocks to get to it and they did the best milkshakes in those tall glasses with shiny cherries and a little straw –

Mila   Those little straws are actually really bad for the /
environment.

Lorna (*snaps*)   Environment, yep, well we know now but we
didn't know then. Anyway, the view from the top was
amazing. You could see the whole of the bay. And everything
just sort of made sense from up there. Being above
everything had this way of making things feel, I don't know
– possible. Me, Mum and Claire would go up – well, Claire
complained the whole time that her feet hurt, so she'd
mostly just wait at the bottom. But I loved it. Told myself I
was going to run it one day, the café. I wanted to live in one
of these little flats here, on the front, so I could just wake up,
walk up the rocks to work and see that view every day.

Mila   Why did they knock it down?

Lorna   Some rich twats built a load of apartments behind it.

Mila   Why didn't you do it? Run it.

Lorna *scoffs.*

Mila   Can't be that hard.

Lorna   Life happened. You happened.

Mila   Soz, Mother.

Lorna   Don't. Not today.

Beat.

Mila   OK, good, well now you've had your little sit down –

Lorna   No, I / need –

Mila   Can we just get on with this, please?

They resume. **Mila** *settles on a spot. She starts playing 'Out of Reach'
by Gabrielle (or another well-known song of hers) through her phone.*

Lorna   Do we really need a soundtrack? Especially
Gabrielle.

Mila   Well Nan loved her and it's not about you, so.

Mila *takes a deep breath and centres herself. She brings out a speech that she's written.*

Mila (*reading*)   You know those headbands they used to sell in the gift shop here? The ones that had your name on them? I always wanted one. And every year, I'd come back, desperate to find one with my name on it, but I never did. And then one year, I told Nan about it, and she went in and said to this woman who worked there, 'We'd like a headband with Mila on it, please' and the woman said, 'We don't have a Mila but we've got a Mia?' So Nan went, 'Her name is *Mila*.' And this woman looked at us, like we were a proper inconvenience, so Nan grabbed the Mia headband, reached behind the till for a pen and added an L to it. It looked shit but she said it didn't matter. Said we had to speak up. Fight for what's right. Even if it's with a shitty headband. And I (*She struggles.*) I really wish that . . . she was still . . .

Mila's *choked up.* **Lorna** *is finding this tricky for her own personal reasons.*

Mila (*quietly*)   You can do your speech now.

Lorna   I didn't know I was meant to have a speech.

Mila   Course you're meant to have a speech. That's what you do when you scatter ashes.

Lorna   There's no set way. You just do what you want to do.

Mila   And I want us to do a speech. Just think of something.

Lorna *tries to speak but nothing really comes out.*

Mila   Anything.

Beat.

How can you not think of anything nice to say about your own mum?

Lorna   Mila, she liked you more than she did me.

Mila   Forget it.

Mila *turns the music off.*

11

Beach

Lorna *is trying to set up a camera timer up on her phone.* **Mila**'s *FaceTiming Courtney.*

Mila (*Facetiming*)   Show me then . . . (*She laughs.*) Chicago Pizza as well. Not even like Papa Johns. You lot are dirty. Literally one night away from home and you're going on like you're Freshers . . . (*She laughs.*)

Lorna *works it out.*

Mila (*FaceTiming*)   Wait, isn't Layla a vegan?

Lorna   Mila.

Mila (*FaceTiming*)   Oh my god, that girl is so full of shit.

Lorna   Mila!

Mila (*FaceTiming*)   Listen, I'll call you back later, yeah? Yeah . . . OK . . . Bye bye bye.

Mila's *demeanour instantly changes.*

Lorna   You know them jumping photos? Where it captures you mid air. Loads of people do it on beaches, I swear there's a name for them –

Mila   Twats.

Lorna   Adventurists.

The timer starts counting down from ten. **Lorna** *hurries back to* **Mila**.

Lorna   Quick!

Mila *reluctantly gets up. She picks up the bucket.*

Lorna   You don't need the bucket.

Mila   I want her in it.

It's a bit of an excruciating wait. They both jump. **Mila**'s *not enthusiastic whatsoever and is careful due to the bucket.* **Lorna**'s *very enthusiastic which doesn't help with the hangover. She heaves a bit.*

Lorna   Thought that Leg Wobbler was on its way back up then.

Lorna *checks the photo.*

Lorna (*irritated*)   Your feet are still on the ground.

Mila *lies down, unfussed.*

Lorna   Did you jump?

Mila   Yes.

Lorna   All you need to do is –

Lorna *demonstrates a little jump.*

Mila   I know how to jump, Mum.

Lorna *notices* **Mila** *isn't undressed.*

Lorna   Are you not getting changed?

Mila   I am changed.

Lorna   Where's your bikini?

Mila   Forgot it.

Lorna   How can you forget your bikini?

Mila   Just did.

Lorna   They'll have one in one of the shops on the front.

Mila   We're going home tomorrow.

Lorna   Yeah, but not until later on –

Mila   I'm alright –

Lorna   They won't be expensive.

Beat.

Lorna   Mila, you can't lay there in a shorts and t-shirt.

Mila   Why not?

Lorna   Because! You look a bit . . .

Mila   A bit what?

Lorna   Like a 'Dad'.

Mila *rolls her eyes.*

Lorna   You can wear a swimming costume if you're paranoid.

Mila   I'm not paranoid!

Lorna   OK.

Mila   Should I be paranoid?

Lorna   No, I'm just saying. Lots of girls get paranoid on beaches.

Mila *goes back to her phone.*

Lorna   We're never going to win. It's all very well Zoe doing these pep talks or whatever you call them but every single woman I know has body hang ups. It's always been like that. Generation after generation.

Mila   And you're just going to accept that?

Lorna   It's just how it's always been. It'll never change. It's too ingrained.

Mila   In what?

Lorna   I don't know. Our heads. The media. I've tried, believe me, I have, but it's exhausting.

Lorna *brings out some left-over cold chips from her bag.*

Lorna   Love cold chips on a hangover.

Mila's *phone pings.*

Lorna   It's a shame. I was doing well with the whole no carbs before Scarbs.

Mila *looks at her phone – her face lights up.* **Lorna** *subtly clocks it.* **Lorna** *puts a chip in between her eyebrows.*

Lorna   Mila, who am I?

Mila *looks.*

Lorna (*old Yorkshire man impression*)   'Keep t' bloody noise down!'

Mila *laughs.*

Mila   Wonder if he's forgiven you for your little performance last night.

Lorna   I can't believe he's still running that B&B. Genuinely thought he'd died years ago.

Mila   I know, I literally shit myself when I saw him at reception. Thought he'd come back from the dead.

They laugh.

Mila *goes back to typing on her phone.*

Lorna   By the way, you're still using the whole 'literally' thing incorrectly. Unless you did *actually* shit yourself.

Mila*'s too distracted by the messages on her phone to even hear* **Lorna**.

Lorna   So, did you remind Max, then? What he's missing?

Mila *smiles, coyly.*

Lorna   And . . .?

Mila *nods, grinning.*

Lorna   In that case, you are welcome.

Mila *goes back to texting.*

Her phone pings.

She reads it and laughs to herself. **Lorna** *laughs along.*

Lorna   What?

Mila *laughs again.*

Lorna   What did he say?

Mila?

Mila (*still engrossed, smiling*)   Nothing.

12

Arcades

Mila *and* **Lorna** *are on a dance mat. The same retro dance mat music plays. But this time, their stamping / movement is much more in sync.*

13

B&B bedroom

Catchphrase is on the TV. They're getting ready to go out whilst watching it. They try and attempt the answers.

Mila   Jacket potato?

Lorna   Big . . . fat . . . potato?

The answer is revealed.

Mila   Couch Potato.   **Lorna**   Couch Potato.

Lorna   Eh, I got an answer right on University Challenge the other night.

Mila   Since when do you watch University Challenge?

Lorna   On Gogglebox. None of the teams got it right though. *And* they were from Oxford and Cambridge.

Mila   Alright, Billy Big Balls. No one likes a know it all.

Lorna   They do, they bloody love them on that show.

Mila   What was the question?

Lorna   Can't remember. Something to do with the Spice Girls.

Mila   Who are they?

Lorna   That's not even funny.

Mila *smiles.*

Lorna   How do you do your flicks like that?

Lorna *gestures to her eyes.*

Mila   I'll show you. Close your eyes.

Mila *delicately helps her with her eye make-up. When she's finished,* **Lorna** *looks in the mirror, satisfied.*

Mila   Like your dress by the way.

Lorna   Charity shop.

Mila*'s impressed.*

Lorna   Just doing my bit for the planet.

Mila *gets a FaceTime call. She looks at it and leaves it.*

Lorna   Courtney?

Mila   I'll call her back later.

Lorna   Gino's isn't booked till eight.

Mila   I know but.

Thought we could have a drink before.

Lorna *stops in her tracks.*

Lorna   A drink?

Mila   Yeah.

Lorna   What, me and you?

Mila   Yeah.

Lorna *beams.*

Lorna   Right! OK! Well, we've got that prosecco. It's only the cheap stuff from Lidl, but.

Mila *shrugs.*

Lorna *excitedly opens the prosecco.* **Mila** *grabs the mugs.* **Lorna** *pours.* **Mila** *toasts.*

Mila   Happy holiday.

Lorna *beams.*

Lorna   Happy holiday!

They drink.

Mila   God that's awful.   **Lorna**   Absolutely horrendous.

14

Gino's restaurant

Lorna *and* **Mila** *sit at a table opposite each other. They're sharing a bottle of wine. The bucket's on the table.*

Lorna (*hushed*)   How fancy's this?

Mila *agrees.*

Lorna   Just gonna pop that down there . . .

Lorna *places the bucket on the floor.*

Mila *burps.*

Lorna   Mila!

Mila   Sorry! It were that gross mug of bubbles.

Lorna (*gestures to the wine*)   This is much nicer.

They clink glasses.

Just casually sharing a bottle of (*Puts on a voice.*) Côtes Du Rhône.

Mila *laughs.*

Lorna   I asked for the table by the window but they gave it to him. (*Gestures to the man on the table next to them.*)

(*Discreetly.*) Looks a bit like a fat version of Gordon Ramsay.

Mila *scoffs.*

Lorna   Claire didn't mention all the mirrors. Don't know why they need so many. Feel like I'm in a funhouse.

Mila *studies the menu.* **Lorna** *adjusts her chair to avoid the mirrors.*

Lorna   Have whatever you want, by the way.

Mila   Bit pricey.

Lorna   It's fine, we're celebrating! End of school . . . holiday . . . results . . .

Mila *shoots her a look.*

Mila   Salmon looks good.

Lorna   Ooo, the salmon does look go – Nineteen quid? For a bit of salmon?

Mila   I'll have something else.

Lorna   It better come with chips.

Mila   It's fine.

Lorna   No, no, have the salmon.

Mila   I don't want the salmon.

Lorna   It doesn't! Doesn't even come with chips.

Mila   I'll have the burger.

Lorna   Bloody hell, how many calories?

Mila *looks closer.*

Lorna   I hate it when places include it. Ignorance is bliss.

Mila   Actually, I think I'll have –

Lorna   Have the burger –

Mila   I don't want the burger –

Lorna   Can you just take a photo before I've eaten?

Lorna *hands over her phone and poses with her wine glass.* **Mila** *takes it.*

Lorna   Say something funny.

Mila   What?

Mila's *phone pings*

Lorna   Make me laugh.

Mila   No.

Lorna *pretends to laugh.*

Mila *takes the photo.*

Lorna   Make me laugh. Go on.

Mila *holds a fork above her eyebrows.*

Mila (*old man Yorkshire impression*)   'Keep t' bloody noise down.'

Lorna *laughs.*

Lorna   Went a bit Bolton there.

Mila   How was that Bolton?!

Lorna   You said (*Bolton accent.*) 'Down.'

Mila   I didn't say (*Bolton accent.*) 'Down.'

Lorna   You did!

Mila   Didn't realise it was an audition.

They laugh.

Ping.

Ping.

Ping.

Lorna   Alright, Miss Popular.

Lorna *looks at the photos whilst* **Mila** *checks her phone.*

Lorna   My chin looks horrible in that.

Ping.

Lorna   Just pop it on silent.

Mila *is suddenly completely consumed.*

Lorna *clocks the mirrors again.*

Lorna   Seriously, who wants a reflection when they're eating?

Ping.

What if you're eating a massive . . . (*She trails off.*)

(*Off* **Mila***'s expression.*) Who is it?

Ping.

Mila?

Ping.

What's up?

Oi.

Who is it?

Pings.

I said, put it on silent.

Pings.

Who is it?

Mila!

Mila (*quietly snaps*)   Just leave it.

Pings.

Lorna *grabs* **Mila***'s phone.*

Mila   What do you think you're doing?!

Mila *wrestles the phone out of her mum's hand. But* **Lorna** *sees one of the messages.*

Lorna   Why is she saying that?

Mila *ignores her and remains fixated to her phone.*

Lorna   Mila!

Mila (*snaps*)   Just leave it!

Lorna   Why is she calling you that?

Silence.

Mila, why is she saying that?

Beat.

Mila (*quietly*)   She's seen the photo.

Lorna   What photo?

Mila   The one I sent to Max.

Lorna   How's *Courtney* seen it?

Mila   She says they've all seen it.

Lorna   I mean, it's just a . . . hang on, what sort of photo is it?

Mila *can't meet her mum's eye.*

Lorna   Mila, what sort of photo is it?

They sit in silence.

Surely it's against the law to share . . . certain . . . / photos –

Mila   No one cares about the law, Mum.

Lorna *goes to make a call.*

Lorna   I'm calling Auntie Claire.

Mila   Why?!

Lorna   She'll know. She's a lawyer.

Mila   Yeah. In property! Don't! Please. Don't.

Lorna *puts her phone down.*

Mila   He's a fucking prick.

Lorna   Look. This will have all blown over by next week.

Mila *scoffs.*

Lorna   Today's news is tomorrow's fish and chip papers. That's what my nan used to say.

Mila   That makes no sense anymore.

Lorna *reaches for* **Mila***'s hand but* **Mila** *pulls it away.*

Lorna   Come on. Don't let this ruin our last night.

Lorna *desperately tries to recover their night.*

Lorna   So, you're having the burger.

Ping.

They also do light bites.

Ping.

And platters.

Ping.

Don't look at it.

Mila *drinks her glass of wine.*

Lorna   Just take that a bit . . . slower.

Mila *continues to drink.*

Ping.

Ping.

Ping.

Lorna *reaches over and grabs the phone.*

Mila   Stop doing that!

Lorna (*hushed*)   Put it on silent.

Mila   Why are you whispering?

Lorna *is very aware of their environment.*

Lorna (*hushed*)   You're being loud.

Mila   So?

Lorna   People are looking.

Mila   Thought you liked it when people looked at you.

Mila *spots the man next to their table looking over.*

Mila (*to the man*)   Is there a problem, or . . .?

Lorna (*hisses*)   What are you doing?

Mila   Yeah, no, it's just – you keep looking at us and it's a bit . . . are you trying to work out what 'this' is? (*Gestures to her and* **Lorna***.*) Because she's white and I'm not? Yeah, we get that a lot.

Lorna (*stern*)   Pack it in.

Mila (*to the man*)   She thinks you look like a fat Gordon Ramsay.

Lorna *is mortified.*

Lorna (*to the man*)   I am so sorry about her –

Everyone is looking at them.

Lorna (*hisses*)   You're embarrassing me.

Mila   You told me to send it.

Lorna *goes to speak but nothing comes out.*

Mila   You told me to send him a photo.

Lorna *looks around and lowers her voice.*

Lorna   I meant, send him a photo of –

Mila   What? Me on the dodgems?

Lorna   No! I –

Mila   You said 'to show him what he's missing'.

Lorna   Yeah, like a photo of you on the beach, or . . . not a photo of your . . . lady bits.

Mila   I didn't send him a photo of my *vagina*, Mum, which you can say by the way, you won't choke. Maybe if you'd normalised the word in the first place –

Lorna   Didn't say 'vagina' enough. I'll add that one to the 'bad mum' list.

Lorna *takes a deep breath.*

Lorna   Let's just take a minute, shall we?

Mila   We? Why do you need 'a' minute? I'm the one that's currently being slut shamed but yeah, you have your minute.

Ping.

Ping.

Ping.

Mila *gets up from the table.*

I feel like I can't breathe.

Lorna (*hushed*)   Sit down.

Mila.

Mila *walks out.*

15

Seafront

It's dark. **Mila** *has climbed up on to the sea railings.* **Lorna** *is behind her on the path.*

Lorna   Can you get down from there, please?

Right, I'm calling a taxi.

Mila   Not getting in. Taxis emit too much carbon.

Lorna   Stop being silly.

Mila   Climate change isn't silly.

Lorna   Just get down! If you slip, that'll be it.

Mila   Oh my god, leave me alone!

Lorna   I'm not leaving you on your own.

Mila   Why? You usually do.

Lorna   No, I / don't!

Mila   You literally left me last night!

Lorna   Yeah, for like an hour –

Mila   The man from the fair.

Skinny Dip Dan.

One ball Paul.

Lorna *can't retaliate.*

Mila   The only reason you're here tonight is because no one's swiped right.

Lorna   OK, that's / enough.

Mila   Why can't you just be alone?

Lorna   I am alone! All the time.

Mila   You're not though, are you? Always finding someone to fill your time with. I actually think being alone would do you some good.

Lorna   Stop talking to me like that.

Mila   Like what?

Lorna   Like you're the mum. I'm the mum.

Mila   You're not a 'mum' though, are you, Lorna?

This stings.

Mila   Courtney's mum folds her washing and cooks her Sunday roasts and takes her shopping for trainers.

Lorna   I've literally taken you on holiday, what more do you want?!

Mila   A weekend in Scarborough is not a holiday.

Lorna   You are so ungrateful. You used to love it here.

Mila   Yeah, when I was a kid.

Lorna   Do you know how much this weekend has cost me? I had to do overtime.

Mila   Good job you like the call centre then.

Lorna   I don't *like* the call centre. I put up with the call centre.

Mila   Get a new job then.

Lorna   Don't tell me to get a new job. You've never even had a job.

Mila   Yeah, because I'm sixteen.

Lorna   I had a job at sixteen –

Mila   You also had a baby at sixteen so forgive me for not following in your footsteps.

Lorna *glares at her.*

Lorna   Do you ever think about how hard this is for me on my own? Putting food on the table, a roof over our heads –

Mila   It's not the eighteen-hundreds Mum, everyone's got roofs –

Lorna   They haven't actually!

Mila   Send me an invoice then.

Lorna   I AM TRYING MY BEST.

Mila   TRY HARDER.

Lorna   You are a *child* who has no idea about the world.

Mila   The world *you've* ruined?

Lorna   Oh god, here we go –

Mila   The world *we* are going to have to fix?

Lorna   It's not *me,* is it? *I've* not ruined it!

Mila   An entire generation which *you* are part of. Nan's / generation –

Lorna   / And it's not ruined –

Mila   The world is on *fire*, Mum. It is literally burning. I'd say that was fucking ruined.

Lorna   Still happy to jet off on a plane to Portugal with your Dad though, aren't you? Where was your Save the Planet placard then?

Mila *can't retaliate.*

Lorna   Stop blaming me for the world we live in.

Mila   Who do I blame then?

Lorna   The government, the social media platforms, the people in charge –

Mila   They're not listening! The world is fucked and nobody is listening.

Lorna   Taking it out on me is not going to help!

Mila   But you could have done your bit. And instead, you've sat on your arse, accepting that plastic's bad for the environment, accepting beach body ready posters, accepting women will just never feel enough – and . . . and not once putting up a fight for any of it. Lazy. You're lazy.

Lorna   Lazy.

Mila   I mean, look at the planet! How did seven billion people let this happen? How can people care about birthdays and weddings and Love Island and not about the pissing planet?

Lorna   You watch Love Island.

Mila   How can you not care?!

Lorna   I cannot just morph into this perfect person you want me to be who has all / the answers.

Mila   It's not about being the perfect person. It's about being real.

Lorna   I am real!

Mila   No you're not. You're constantly trying to get the best angle. Covering our shit up in seasides and fairgrounds and / . . . Leg Wobblers.

Lorna   You put on a 'performance' every time you speak to your friends! 'Nah, seriously, oh my daaaays, siiiiick'. Perhaps you should try being real before you lecture me about it.

Mila   How can I be real when my own mum filters me?

Lorna *opens her mouth to speak.*

Mila   You filter every single photo you take of me.

You trying to make me look lighter or something? So, we can really look like mum and daughter?

Lorna   That is too far.

Mila   You take these photos of yourself, trying to portray to the world that you're happy –

Lorna   I *am* happy!

Mila   You can't eat in a room if there's a mirror. You haven't cried about Nan. Every time I mention Dad, you flinch. / Even though you broke up years ago.

Lorna   How dare you speak to me like that?

Mila   Because you ruin my life!

Lorna   Yeah, well you ruined mine.

They're seething.

This whole trip, I have just wanted to celebrate you leaving school, a new chapter for you, your exams – but do you know what? I don't care. No one cares. No one will even bother to ask you about your GCSEs in a few months. And there you are, being so bloody precious about it (*Mocking voice.*) 'Oh I'm not telling you my results, I'm not telling you, I'm not telling anyone' –

Mila   I told Dad.

They stare at each other.

Lorna   I have tried so hard to raise you with / as much –

Mila   You didn't raise me. Nan did.

This stings even more.

Mila   She took me to school, did my homework with me, put me to bed.

She did so much for me and all you did was take her for granted. You don't realise how lucky you were to have her.

I wish she'd have been my mum. She was so much more of a mum to me than you.

Lorna *snaps.*

Lorna   Your nan physically threw me out on to the street when I was having you.

Mila   Here we go –

Lorna   She wasn't always this saint you paint her / out to be.

Mila   Oh my god, she threw you out because you got yourself knocked up at fifteen – get over it.

Lorna   She threw me out because you weren't going to be white.

Silence.

Mila *suddenly laughs.*

Mila   You're a fucking liar.

They're unable to speak. It's very uncomfortable for a moment.

Lorna   I – I didn't – I didn't / mean for –

Mila   She's gone.

Lorna (*very gentle*)   I know. And I know it's hard –

Mila   No – she's literally gone.

Lorna *realises the bucket's disappeared.*

Lorna   Where did you last have it?

Mila   I –

Lorna   Gino's. You had the bucket in Gino's.

Mila   We have to go back –

Lorna   We're not going back tonight.

Mila   We have to!

Lorna   Look, tonight has been a lot and –

Mila   You didn't fight for her when she was alive so I suppose why would you now she's dead?

Lorna (*quietly*)   Enough. I think we've both said enough.

Mila   You love the enoughs don't you? I don't smile
enough. I'm not fun enough. Don't dance enough. Not thin
enough. Not curvy enough. Not white enough. Not black
enough. / Not clever enough –

Lorna   I didn't mean you! I'm saying enough / as in–

Mila   I clearly wasn't enough before I was even born, so
how the fuck am I meant to stand a chance now?

Lorna *goes to embrace* **Mila** *but she pushes her away.*

And the sun falls from the sky.

Sunday

16

B&B bedroom

It's very late / very early.

Lorna *is alone.*

She turns the TV on. And then turns it off again.

She's horribly restless.

She attempts to call **Mila** *again.*

17

Mila *listens to her answerphone messages.*

Nan Mila? Oh, I thought you'd picked up. (*She laughs.*) I'll try you in a bit –

Nan Mila, it's Nan – I've tried you on WhatsApp but I'm only getting one tick – just to say you can come over whenever you finish. My doctor's appointment's been pushed back until next week now – NHS is on its bloody knees. Anyway, I've got those Kiev things in you like. They were on offer at the Co-op, three for two, so. Anyway, I know you don't like waffly messages, so – see you soon. Love you.

Lorna Mila, I – I think Monobrow Bob's locked the front door, and I – I don't want you to be cold, stood out the front. So let me know when you're back and I'll come down. I – please come back. I know I – I just – I want to explain – I really didn't mean for it to – I was just trying to protect – anyway. I'm not doing this on here. I know you don't like waffly messages, so – see you soon. Love you.

Nan Mila? Oh, I thought you'd picked up. (*She laughs.*) I'll try you in a bit–

Nan   Mila? Oh, I thought you'd picked up. (*She laughs.*) I'll try you in a bit –

Nan   Mila? Oh, I thought you'd picked up. (*She laughs.*) I'll try you in a bit –

18

B&B bedroom

Mila *zips up her case.* **Lorna** *watches her.*

Lorna   Check out's not until eleven.

Mila   Dad said I could just come whenever, so.

Lorna *nods, trying to disguise her disappointment.*

Lorna   Didn't wake you this morning, did I?

Mila *shakes her head.*

Lorna   Thought it was best to let you sleep.

Mila   Don't even know what time I / got back.

Lorna   Three forty-two. Ish.

Beat.

Lorna   Have you eaten?

Mila *shakes her head.*

Lorna *grabs a load of custard creams by the kettle.*

Lorna   May as well. Paid premium for them.

Mila *fills her pockets.*

There's an awkward silence between them.

Lorna   I, um. I couldn't really sleep, so ended up walking to Gino's first thing.

Lorna *picks up the bucket from the side of her bed and pops it on the side.*

It was still under the table.

Mila   She.

Lorna   No. *It.*

Lorna *hesitates.*

I'm sorry but I can't – to me, my mum is –

She starts again.

My mum isn't *that.*

A mutual understanding.

Think I really freaked the poor cleaner out trying to explain what I was looking for.

Lorna *smiles, weakly.*

You got everything?

Mila *nods.*

Lorna   What time's your train?

Mila   On the hour.

Lorna   And your dad's going to fetch / you from . . .?

Mila *nods.*

Lorna   Mila, I know nothing I say will . . . but literally the second your nan met you, she loved you more than she loved anyone. Ever.

Beat.

To avoid becoming upset, **Mila** *goes to leave.*

Mila   See you then.

She takes the bucket and leaves.

Lorna *stands alone in the space.*

Her world crumbles.

Suddenly **Mila** *walks back in.*

Mila (*gestures to the bucket*)   It's actually quite annoying to carry with my case.

Lorna   I can (take it)

Mila   Makes sense to . . . Whilst we're here. She did love it here.

Beat.

Lorna   Any idea where you want to . . .?

Mila   She liked the Ferris wheel.

Lorna   Nice try.

19

The top of the hill

A moment as they catch their breath from walking up. They look out at the bay.

Mila   You can see our B&B.

Lorna   You can see everything.

Mila *takes out a biscuit from her pocket and eats a bit of it.*

Mila   I got nine grade 6s by the way.

Lorna   Wait, are they Bs?

Mila (*exasperated*)   How many times. They're numbers now.

Lorna   You got nine Bs?!

Mila *rolls her eyes and nods.*

Lorna *tries to contain her excitement.*

Lorna   That is . . . bloody hell, well / done!

Mila   I was predicted four grade 8s.

Lorna's *thrown.*

Mila   As.

Lorna   So? They're still really good grades!

Mila *is clearly disappointed.*

Lorna   That doesn't affect sixth form does it or –

Mila *shakes her head.*

Mila   Just thought I'd do better.

Lorna   You've done great! Look – I've got goosebumps.

Lorna *shows her.*

Mila   I thought you 'didn't care'.

She shrugs it off.

Lorna   I was just playing it cool.

They smile weakly.

Lorna   Look, I want to say something, before we . . . um
– (scatter)

Mila   Like a speech?

Lorna   Yeah.

Mila   Shall I play Gabrielle?

Lorna   No.

Think I'll close my eyes.

Mila   Why?

Lorna   It's just easier.

Lorna *closes her eyes. She struggles to get the words out at points.
This is the first time we've seen* **Lorna** *both nervous and emotional.
She opens her eyes at some point throughout the speech but never
once looks at* **Mila***.*

Lorna   When I found out I was having you, I felt like I
didn't . . . When me and your dad split up, I didn't think I'd

done . . . Every time I try on a pair of shorts in H&M, it's like I don't feel . . . (*She becomes frustrated at not being able to get the words out.*) And I'm bored. I am thirty-two and I am so bored of feeling like this. And you are *not* going to feel the same. Because you're brilliant. You're good with money, you untangle jewellery quicker than I've ever known anyone to, you match Tuppaware with the right lids, and – and – I know I should have said all this sooner – and not to sound like I'm getting the violins out or anything, but no one ever told me. That I was brilliant. And I know I don't always give you the best advice, and I'm shit with money, and I tell you my clothes are from charity shops when they're actually from Primark – but I – I find being a mum really hard. And I feel like I'm not meant to say that, but . . . And I know I should be setting some sort of example, but it feels impossible in a society that's been designed to constantly make us – not feel enough. So, at some point, we just have to say fuck this, you know? Sorry – for saying the f word – again – but yeah, fuck this. Because life is short and we don't how long we've got, and – and I just –what's that song by Lady Gaga – 'Born This Way' – I mean, I know she's not aimed it at two women from Sheffield, well, who knows, maybe she has, I don't know what I'm on about now, I've gone off on a tangent about Lady Gaga, but basically what I'm saying is I second guess myself with everything – literally every single decision I make – but the one thing I am certain of – the one thing I really do know, is that you are enough. More than enough. And I promise to try and remind you – us – more.

Neither of them have the words.

Lorna *gestures it's time.* **Mila** *takes a deep breath and turns the bucket upside down. For a moment, they observe.*

Mila   Thanks for . . . what you said.

Beat.

Apart from the bit about Tuppaware. That's not a compliment. Anyone can do that.

Lorna   You'd be surprised.

Beat.

Have you told your dad? About the . . . whole photo thing?

Mila   Obviously not.

Lorna *nods.*

Lorna   It will get better. I know it really doesn't seem like that now, but . . .

Mila*'s not convinced.*

Mila   Anyway, I'd better . . .

Lorna   OK.

Mila *goes to leave but stops.*

Mila   I thought I'd feel happier after – but now, it's like – she's really gone.

Beat.

Lorna   When my nan died, I remember my mum saying to me that for as long as I was around, my nan would be too. Because she could see so much of her in me. And I never truly understood what she meant, but . . . now, I –

She looks at **Mila**. *She confirms.*

A moment.

Mila   I won this for you, by the way. On the slots.

Mila *brings out a small rubber from her pocket and hands it over.*

When I say won, I mean I spent five bloody quid worth of 2ps on it.

Lorna *studies it.*

Lorna   Sorry, what is it?

Mila   I don't really know. I mean, it's a rubber but . . . a pea maybe? Or a sprout? They didn't have any mushrooms.

Lorna's *really touched by the thought.*

Mila   Also, I was thinking about what you said, about mushrooms having awful lives and I think you're wrong.

Lorna's *put out.*

Mila   OK, mushrooms are shat on every day, but without the shit, they literally wouldn't grow, would they?

Floored.

Mila   God, I am so wise.

Lorna   Alright, Billy Big Balls. No one likes a know it all.

Mila   Soz, Mother.

Lorna *shoots her a look.*

They breathe Scarborough in. In this moment, everything is peaceful.

And then **Mila** *holds* **Lorna**'s *hand.*

End.